let's
Cook

Ivan Bulloch & Diane James

WORLD BOOK / TWO-CAN

LS MS

Art Director: Ivan Bulloch
Editor: Diane James
Design Assistant: Peter Clayman
Illlustrator: Emily Hare
Photographer: Daniel Pangbourne
Models: Courtney, Natalia, Jonathan, Grant,
Kaz, Alicia, Stephanie
Special thanks to: Karen Ingebretsen, World Book Publishing

First published in the United States and Canada in 1997 by
World Book, Inc.
525 W. Monroe
20th Floor
Chicago, IL USA 60661
in association with Two-Can Publishing Ltd.

**For information on other World Book products,
call 1-800-255-1750, x 2238.**

ISBN: 0-7166-5600-0 (hbk)
ISBN: 0-7166-5601-9 (pbk)
LC: 96-61754

Printed in Spain

1 2 3 4 5 6 7 8 9 10 01 00 99 98 97 96

Contents

4...ready, set, go

6...dips

8...perfect pasta

10...make a pizza

12...stuffed potatoes

14...choco-licious

16...ginger cookies

18...chilly treats

20...shake and sip

22...party time

24...tips and tricks

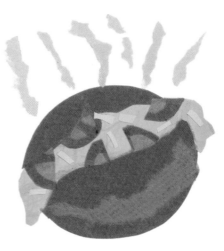

ready, set, go

The great thing about preparing food is that you can share the fun! Friends and family will appear out of nowhere to sample your treats! So get cooking (but be sure to have a grown-up help you with the tricky parts).

get ready
mixing bowls
saucepans
measuring cup
rolling pin
strainer, sieve
kitchen scale
whisk, grater, fork
chopping knife
chopping board
can opener
wooden spoon
icing bag
oven mitts
teaspoon (tsp)
tablespoon (tbsp)

Grown-up help with Knives

1 Safety first!
There are a few simple rules to follow when cooking. First, never use a knife by yourself. Ask a grown-up to help. There will be plenty of things for you to do!

Grown-up help with Stove

2 Be careful with heat!
Pots and baking pans can get very, very hot. Always have a grown-up with you when you are using an oven or stove and don't touch anything hot unless you are wearing oven mitts!

3 Say NO to germs!
When you are working with food, it's very important that you have clean hands! Also keep your hair tied back or wear a real chef's hat!

Wash your hands

4 Neat and tidy
Get your equipment and ingredients together before you start. When you've finished, wash everything up and put it away.

come on, let's get cracking!

dips

What do you do if some hungry friends come over to see you, and it's not time for lunch or supper? Why not prepare a delicious, quick snack? Our yummy dip is similar to a salad that is popular in Greece!

shopping list (for 6)
1 cucumber
small bunch of mint
1 large container of
   yogurt
bag of tortilla chips

get ready
chopping knife
chopping board
mixing bowl
wooden spoon

2 Take a small handful of mint and strip the leaves off the main stalk. Bunch them together and cut them carefully into small shreds.

1 Cut the cucumber in half and then into long, thin lengths. Next, chop the strips into really small square shapes.

3 Empty the yogurt into a mixing bowl. Mix in the chopped cucumber and shredded mint leaves. That's one dip, now try another!

4 You could mix ketchup with yogurt and add thinly chopped onion. Or mix cream cheese with chives. Serve your favorite dip with a mountain of tortilla chips or potato chips.

better try it myself first!

perfect pasta

Here's a pasta treat for summer days. It will take only a few minutes to put the ingredients together. Then you can enjoy eating your special pasta salad in the sunshine.

shopping list (for 4)
1/2 lb. (225g) pasta
1 orange pepper
3 tomatoes
4 green onions
sweet corn
raisins
parsley

get ready
large saucepan
oven mitts
strainer
chopping knife
chopping board
mixing bowl
wooden spoon
tablespoon

1 Put plenty of water in a saucepan and bring to a boil. Read the instructions on the pasta package to find out how long to cook it. Pour the pasta into the boiling water.

2 Ask a grown-up to cook the pasta and strain it for you. Keep the pasta in the strainer and rinse it with cold water. Shake the strainer from side to side to get rid of all the water.

3 Chop up the pepper, onion, and tomatoes on a chopping board.

4 When the pasta is cold, mix it with the chopped vegetables in a big bowl. Then add a few spoonfuls of raisins and sweet corn.

5 Stir in your favorite salad dressing. You could try mayonnaise with a little ketchup, a mixture of oil and vinegar, or just some olive oil with a little lemon juice. Chop the parsley and sprinkle it on the top.

there's too much just for me!

make a pizza

Everyone loves a slice of yummy pizza with gooey melted cheese. And the best thing about a pizza treat is that you can share it with your friends! How many different toppings can you make up?

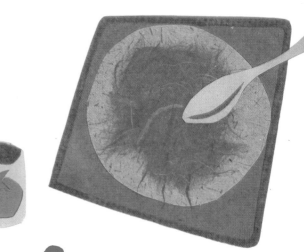

shopping list (for 4)
2 green peppers
1 onion
four mushrooms
canned sweet corn
9 oz. (250g) mozzarella
1 large pizza crust
1 can of tomato sauce

get ready
chopping knife
chopping board
baking pan
wooden spoon
oven mitts
mixing bowl

1 Cut up the mushrooms, peppers, and mozzarella. Slice the onion thinly. Save the leftovers to make a refreshing side salad to eat with your pizza.

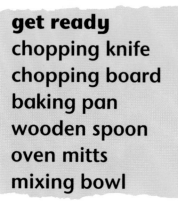

2 Put the pizza crust on a baking pan and spoon on the tomato sauce. Use the back of the spoon to smooth it out evenly, not quite to the edges.

3 Arrange all the sliced ingredients on top of the tomato sauce, starting with the mozzarella. Finish with spoonfuls of corn.

4 Read the instructions on the pizza crust package. They will tell you how hot the oven should be and how long to cook the pizza.

hurry up, don't let it get cold!

stuffed potatoes

Baked potatoes are great when you are feeling hungry! There are dozens of different fillings to choose from. Have a competition with your friends to see who can come up with the most unusual ingredients.

this looks big enough

shopping list (for 4)
4 medium potatoes
4 oz. (100g) cheese
2 tomatoes
butter or margarine
1 can of tuna
$\frac{1}{2}$ cucumber
1 tbsp mayonnaise

get ready
baking dish
oven mitts
chopping board
mixing bowl, grater
knife, fork
tablespoon

1 Set the oven to 375°F. (190°C). Scrub the potatoes to get the dirt off. Put them on a baking pan and prick them with a fork. Cook the potatoes for about 1 hour.

pick a perfect potato!

2 To make a delicious cheese filling, grate some hard cheese and mix it with chopped tomato.

4 When the potatoes are cooked, cut each one in half and scoop out the inside. Mix the cooked potato with several pats of butter and add some filling. Pile the mix back into the skin. It's ready to eat!

3 Try a mixture of tuna, chopped cucumber, and a spoonful of mayonnaise.

choco-licious

Try to keep your fingers out of the bowl when you are making this delicious chocolate mousse! If you keep tasting, there won't be any left for your friends.

shopping list (for 4)
5 oz. (150g) semisweet
    chocolate
3 eggs

get ready
mixing bowls
saucepan
fork
wooden spoon
oven mitts
whisk

2 Put a little water in a saucepan and rest a mixing bowl snugly on top. Break the chocolate into the bowl, and have a grown-up help you melt the chocolate over low heat while you stir it.

1 Crack the eggs open carefully. Put the yolks in one bowl and the whites in another. Don't mix them! Beat the yolks with a fork.

3 Turn off the heat and add the egg yolks to the melted chocolate. Mix everything up well and let it cool for about 10 minutes. Lift the bowl out.

14

4 Whisk the egg whites until they are stiff and stand in little peaks. Nearly there!

everybody loves chocolate!

5 Carefully fold the egg whites into the chocolate mixture. Then pour it all into a big serving bowl. Refrigerate it until it is set.

6 You can serve your chocolate mousse as it is, or decorate it with whipped cream and colored candies.

ginger cookies

These delicious ginger cookies are not difficult to make – and even easier to eat! Make a batch and put some in a box for a special friend.

shopping list
- ½ cup (115g) brown sugar
- ½ cup (115g) butter
- 1 egg
- 1 ½ cups (200g) flour
- ½ tsp baking soda
- 1 tsp ground ginger
- ready-made icing

get ready
- mixing bowl
- wooden spoon
- sieve
- rolling pin
- baking pan
- cookie cutters
- oven mitts

1 Beat the sugar and butter together in a large bowl until the mixture is fluffy. Separate the yolk from the white of the egg. Mix the white into the sugar and butter and beat until it's all mixed together.

2 Put a sieve over the bowl and sift in the flour, ginger, and baking soda. Mix everything together to make a slightly stiff dough.

3 Wrap the dough in plastic wrap and refrigerate it an hour. Sprinkle flour on the work surface and roll out the dough until it's about ¼ in. (5mm) thick.

come and get it!

they're yummy!

4 Use your cutters to cut shapes out of the dough. Put them on a greased baking pan and bake at 350°F (180°C) for 10 to 12 minutes.

5 If you like, you can decorate your cookies with icing and candies when they are cool. Ready-made icing in squeezable tubes will make the job fun!

chilly treats

Ice cream tastes great all year round, but it's especially good for cooling you down on hot days. Pop a batch in the freezer and invite your friends over. Our simple recipe uses yogurt as a base. Choose your favorite flavorings and get mixing!

2 Empty the container of yogurt into a mixing bowl. Add the chopped fruit and stir with a wooden spoon.

shopping list (for 4)
16 oz. (450g) candied
    fruit, red and green
1 large container
    plain yogurt

1 Chop the candied fruit into small pieces. (You can find it in the baking section of most supermarkets.)

get ready
chopping board
knife, wooden spoon
mixing bowl
plastic container

3 Pour the mixture into the plastic container. Put the container in the freezer. It's looking good!

4 After an hour or two, the edges should be frozen over. Pour the half-frozen mix back into a bowl and stir it up again. Then put it back in the freezer.

5 After another hour your frozen yogurt should be ready to eat. You could serve it with cookies, or in tall glasses with a spoonful of whipped cream!

a spoonful for me...

...and one for me

shake and sip

What could be more delicious than a frothy, fruity smoothie? Follow these simple instructions and you'll soon be sipping a refreshing strawberry treat. How about a banana shake for dessert?

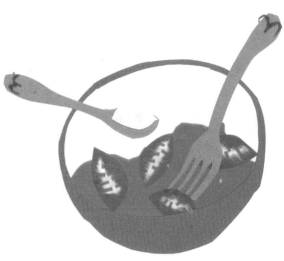

shopping list (for 2)
2 cups (500ml) milk
6 strawberries
1 tsp sugar

get ready
chopping board
chopping knife
fork
jar with screw top
glass
straw

1 Twist the green tops off the strawberries. Cut the strawberries into slices to make them easier to mash up. Put the slices into a mixing bowl.

2 Add a teaspoon of sugar to the strawberries in the bowl. Mash everything up together.

3 Put the strawberry mash into a screw top jar. Add the milk, leaving a little space at the top of the jar.

mmmm...perfect for a sunny day

Shake

Shake

4 Screw the top on tightly. Now shake as hard as you possibly can, up and down and side to side. Pour the mixture into a large glass and enjoy it. Sip your foamy drink through a straw!

21

party time

What's the best thing about a party? The cake, of course! You can buy a cake from the store and make it look great by decorating it with colored icing and adding candies and candles.

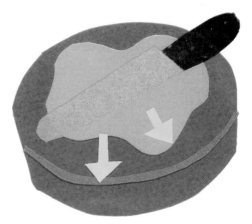

shopping list
for water icing
1 cup (225g) powdered sugar
water, food coloring
for butter icing
1/2 cup (125g) butter
1 cup (225g) powdered sugar
food coloring

get ready
spatula
mixing bowls
wooden spoon
tablespoon
icing bag and nozzle

1 Make some water icing to cover the cake. Put the powdered sugar in a mixing bowl and add water one tablespoon at a time. Mix well until the mixture is smooth and creamy. Add a few drops of food coloring.

2 Use a spatula to spread the water icing over the top of the cake. Don't worry if it slips down the sides as well. Leave the icing to dry.

3 Now make some butter icing to decorate your cake! Chop the butter into small pieces and mix it with the powdered sugar. Stir the mixture until it is smooth. Stir in a few drops of food coloring.

4 Fill an icing bag half full of butter icing. Screw on a star-shaped nozzle.

5 Hold the top of the bag closed with one hand and squeeze out icing stars with the other. Top your cake with candies and candles.

happy birthday to me!

tips and tricks

Here are some of our favorite tips to help you become a first-class cook!

1 Add a teaspoon of oil to the water when you are cooking pasta. It will keep the pasta pieces from sticking together.

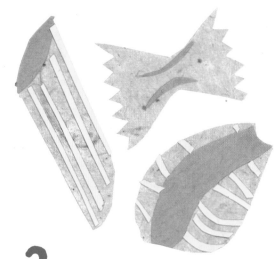

2 Put a clean, folded dish towel under your mixing bowl. It will keep it from slipping all over the place.

3 Make your food look as exciting as possible. Even the plainest food tastes better if it looks good!

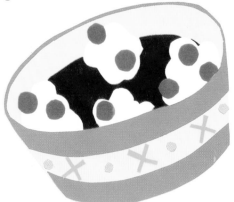

4 Save plastic containers with lids. They are useful for storing leftovers.

5 Instead of chips, try serving cut-up carrots, celery, or zucchini with dip. It's a healthful and colorful treat.

6 Keep a cookbook with your favorite recipes in it.